cellar

for Matthew Cartwright
+ Peter MacQueen

in celebration of a decade building cellars together
and a lifetime enjoying their contents

cellar

Tyson Stelzer

WINE PRESS

cover: The Drives at Seppelt Great Western in Central Victoria. The 2.5km network of tunnels was dug by gold miners in the late 1860s.

WINE PRESS
Brisbane, Australia
www.winepress.com.au
cellar@winepress.com.au

First published in Australia by Wine Press 2007

National Library of Australia Cataloguing-in-Publication data:

Stelzer, Tyson, 1975- .
Cellar.
Includes index.
ISBN 0 9775548 1 3.
1. Wine - Storage - Australia. 2. Wine cellars - Australia.
I. Title.
641.220994

Cover photography and design by Tyson Stelzer
Typesetting and layout by Wine Press
Photography and artwork by Tyson Stelzer.
Proudly printed in Australia by Openbook Australia, Adelaide.

All 240V electrical work referred to in this book must be attempted by a qualified electrician. Every effort has been made to ensure that the principles and procedures outlined represent the best practice in the field. However, the author accepts no responsibility for any consequences resulting from their interpretation.

No one after drinking old wine
wants the new, for he says,
'The old is better.'

Jesus, Luke 5:39

Tyson Stelzer is co-author, with UK wine writer Matthew Jukes, of the best-selling book *Taste Food & Wine: Choose the right wine every time.* He was a contributor to the third edition of *The Oxford Companion to Wine* and the author of *Cellaring Wine: Do-it-yourself solutions, Screwed for Good? The case for screw caps on red wines, Seal of Approval: Why choose screw caps?* and *Taming the Screw: A manual for winemaking with screw caps.* Tyson writes a monthly wine column for *Brisbane Style* and *Style South* magazines and contributes to numerous wine magazines as well as his online wine guide, www.tysonstelzer.com. He has presented at wine conferences in the United Kingdom, Japan, South Africa, New Zealand and Australia. The co-creator with Matthew Jukes of *The Great Australian Red* – the quest for the best Shiraz/Cabernet, Tyson was also a finalist for the 2006 *International Wine and Spirit Competition's Communicator of the Year.*

contents

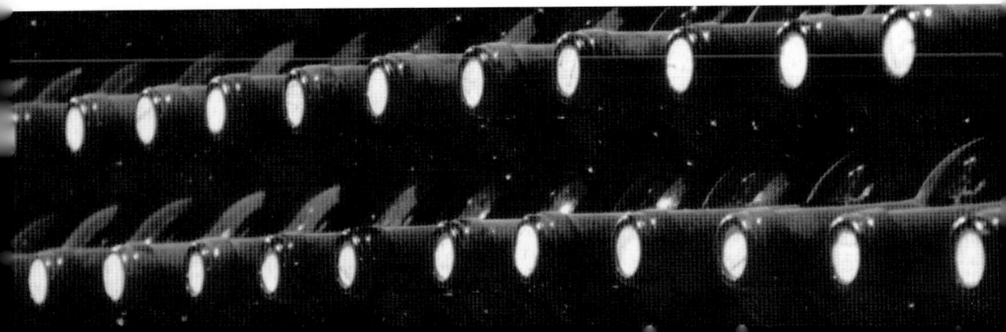

by the same author

The wine world is on the move like never before. Changes are at hand that affect what you drink, how you drink and even how you should handle and store your wines.

Since the release of the prequel to this book, *Cellaring Wine: do-it-yourself solutions*, four years ago, a lot of wine has flown under the bridge. Today, a massive grape glut has driven the rise of the ubiquitous "clean skin," while the steady ascent in quality of "labelled" bottles has kept discerning consumers thoroughly delighted. We now have access to more outstanding wines than ever before – and at more competitive prices.

There are a number of reasons for this. First, a rising interest in fine food and a fascination with international cuisine have seen more discerning and more adventurous consumers push up the demand for quality wines from abroad, fuelling a steady flow of bottles to our shores from every wine-producing corner of the planet. More significant than this has been the upward spiral of our own wines, now internationally regarded among the best quality and value on earth. Increased demand in a rapidly growing industry has kept quality buoyant, as has the ever-rising standard of fruit as the burgeoning plantings of the 1990s come to maturity. The dynamic body of winemakers across the country has risen to this challenge, with more talented makers and more sheer passion and enthusiasm than ever. Australian wine is white-hot right now.

The winner, of course, is the consumer. We are presented with shelf after shelf of brilliant options every time we step into a bottle shop or restaurant. At the same time, we are now confronted with another choice unfamiliar to most of us four years ago.

The adoption of superior closure technologies for wine bottles represents the most significant quality gain of the modern wine industry. The variabilities of traditional corks and their ill-effects on bottled wine are becoming a thing of the past as they're replaced with more dependable closures. The screw

cap is the most reliable of these, with proven performance in wine quality, consistency and ageability.

The implications of these modern revolutions in closure technology and wine quality are far-reaching, but nowhere else are they as profound as they are in the cellar. As quality spirals higher and prices plummet lower, we have within our reach more eminently age-worthy wines at keen prices than ever before. Meanwhile, screw caps change the rules of cellaring almost entirely, moving the goal posts further apart and giving punters a greater chance of scoring on every attempt. Home cellaring has never been more promising.

Nor has it been easier. If your vision of a wine cellar is a dark, musty hole in the ground frequented by dilapidated bottles, wine snobs and the occasional cellar rat, you're in for a pleasant surprise. Wine cellars are now high-tech gear, and they're appealing to a whole new generation. Cellars today rely on air-conditioning and refrigeration – the cost of which has plummeted in the past four years, making a climate-controlled cellar a feasible option for everyone. Today, you can buy a wine "fridge" from virtually any department store, and often for under $200. A small air conditioner, capable of transforming any small room into a cellar, will not set you back much more.

Wine cellars are now high-tech gear, and they're appealing to a whole new generation

The combined effect of these changes is nothing less than a revolution in home cellaring. And Australians have never been more interested. When I self-published *Cellaring Wine: do-it-yourself* solutions four years ago, I never expected that it would be featured in almost every wine magazine and capital city newspaper in Australia, prime-time radio and television. Four years later, the third print run has sold out and demand remains as high as ever.

A simple reprint or second edition would not do justice to the vast range of home cellaring possibilities now at hand. It was clear that a complete rewrite was in order, maintaining the practical relevance of the first book, but extending it beyond "do-it-yourself solutions" to embrace the full scope of this ever-evolving pursuit.

The result is *Cellar*. I wish you as much fun with these ideas as I have had creating them.

introduction

This book is about making the most of every bottle you drink. Some wines are best enjoyed young and fresh, while others benefit from the opportunity to mature and grow.

Buying wine can be a bit like buying a new plant from the nursery. Sometimes you bring it home for a special occasion, put it on display for a short time and its job is done. No fuss, no stress, and if it's dead the next day no one really cares. But other times you're not buying it for what it represents right now. You know that with a little care and nurture it will blossom into something much greater.

Wine is capable of miraculous transformations in the cellar. My fascination with this began a decade ago with a humble case of 1995 Orlando Jacob's Creek Shiraz Cabernet. This was quite an investment for a student, and the case gained pride of place in the bottom corner of my parents' linen cupboard. Bottle after bottle, month after month, year after year, I was amazed at the way it developed and evolved. The last two bottles of the case survived in the cupboard for three years, and they were the best of the lot. Despite the $6.50 price tag of this humble commercial wine from an average vintage, it had integrated and developed nicely after just a few years in relatively poor storage.

At the other end of the price ladder, it was around the same time that I first tasted Penfolds Grange from the same vintage. Far too young to be drunk at the time, I was left wondering what all the hype was about.

The following year my curiosity was aroused by an unknown wine which was produced by a friend at a dinner party. A big, brooding red wine with impeccable balance and complexity, this was an awe-inspiring experience for a young wine buff. After a few hopeless attempts at guessing its identity, the wine was revealed to be a 1976 Penfolds Grange. At 25 years of age it was still singing, with plenty of voice left in it yet. The cellar had worked its magic. Now I understood.

While the entry-level Jacob's Creek may not be the first thing you'd race out to grab to stock the cellar, and Grange will probably always be out of reach for most of us, between these two extremes lies an ocean of amazing, age-worthy wine awaiting discovery. To enjoy these wines at their best, they're going to need some time in the cellar.

Wines grow up a little like we do. With some patience, they mature to lose their rough edges, and are less likely to grate on your senses. A multi-faceted personality emerges, replacing the simplicity of its youth with a deeper interest. It can become more pleasant company at the table, complementing rather than dominating. White wines tend to relinquish their racy acidity to gloriously rich complexity. In reds, tannins soften as vibrant fruit freshness makes way for a more mature temperament of smooth fruit and mellow richness. Your taste will dictate precisely where in this progression the wine hits its prime. It's a simple matter of drinking it when you like it best.

Sharing a carefully cellared old bottle with family or friends ranks among my favourite things. Striking a dud bottle is right up there with the worst! Over years of enjoying wines stored in perfect cellars, some from less than ideal conditions and the odd random old bottle of unknown origin from auction, the effects of storage conditions on wine quality and development have become painfully obvious. The impact is far more profound than I ever imagined, even while I was writing *Cellaring Wine*. I now understand that the deteriorating effects of poor storage outweigh the benefits of ageing to the point that I would not suggest keeping wine for a long time at all, unless reasonably good cellaring conditions are available. But when they are, the results can be nothing less than glorious.

Setting up the right conditions is not as difficult as you might think. An ideal wine cellar is no longer out of reach for anyone, and by the end of this book you'll be equipped with everything you need to know to create the cellar that's just right for your drinking needs, be it for 3 dozen or 300 dozen bottles. The rewards of well-cellared wine can be yours to enjoy without excessive expense or effort.

When you've seen just how majestic a fully-grown plant can become, you would hardly bring a pot home from the nursery, cut off the flowers, arrange them in a vase and throw away the rest. In the same way, patience with certain wines will be rewarded. Before you can reap this reward, you first need to know how to care for the "plant."

The first step to achieving this is to ensure that you are buying a healthy plant. Make sure your wines are in top condition to start with. This warrants special consideration.

wine transportation and storage: a call for action

We live in a big, hot country and wine often travels long distances and sits in warehouses for extended periods of time. Temperatures on the back of a truck, in the hull of a ship, under the tin roof of a storage facility or on the shelf of a wine shop that isn't climate-controlled can quickly soar, and these conditions take a serious toll on wine quality. Just a few hours roasting on the back of a truck can be enough to destroy a wine forever.

There is a lot more that the Australian wine industry can – and should – be doing to deliver wine to you in pristine condition. This is set to become more important over the coming years. The rising quality and consistency delivered by screw caps, improvements in modern winemaking techniques and diligence in winery hygiene will raise consumer's expectations. Other sources of variability in wine will consequently become all the more obvious, and this is why there will be less tolerance of poor delivery and warehousing conditions in the future.

There is a need in this country for a system in which climate-control is guaranteed at every link in the chain from winery to consumer. This would be a costly operation, and it will only be viable if you are prepared to pay a little more for this luxury. When you're offered the choice, make sure you make the right decision, and don't miss the opportunity to enjoy great wine in perfect condition.

In the meantime, there are a few things that you can do to ensure that your wine arrives in top form. Only shop at wine stores that are climate-controlled 24/7 and that store their wines out the back under similar conditions. If in doubt, ask the manager to show you the cooling system, or look the shop up in the retailer directory in *Taste Food & Wine*, where we review every decent wine store in Australia. When you order directly from the producer or from an online retailer, request climate-controlled shipping (at your cost) or ask them to delay delivery until the cooler months of the year.

Caution is required in purchasing wines imported from afar, as a shipping container exposed to the elements on the deck of a ship is a torture chamber for a bottle of wine. Some importers use refrigerated containers - seek them out and give them your support.

the secrets of the cellar

"We opened a bottle of Penfolds Bin 389 Cabernet Shiraz on the weekend," my friend told me last week. "It was ordinary – I mean really ordinary – a waste of great wine." It seems that a decade without proper cellaring in Queensland had sucked the life out of his poor bottle.

When you bring a plant home from the nursery, the first thing you do is check the tag for the conditions that the plant enjoys, and choose an appropriate location in the garden. You would hardly expect it to survive if you left it in the harshest corner of the yard and neglected to water and fertilise it.

Regrettably, this is just what happened to my friend's 389, and he knew it the moment he poured the first glass. Poorly cellared wine loses its vibrancy, its definition and its finer nuances. It's like listening to your favourite band, but from the next room with the door shut! It's still all there, but a bit flat and boring.

The wine rack in the dining room and the cupboard above the refrigerator are not friendly environments for cellaring wines. Another friend recently showed me a very attractive wine rack that he had built in his new kitchen. After just a few weeks, some of his wines were showing signs of leaking around the corks. Wine responds to the conditions in which it is placed, for better or for worse.

If the plan is to drink it soon, storage locations like those of my friends are probably not too much of a catastrophic concern. But if wines are cellared for the purpose of developing maturity, then the right conditions are absolutely crucial. The difference between a well-cellared wine and a poorly cellared wine can be like comparing a super-premium bottle from a top maker to a cheap cask glugger. It makes that much difference. Seriously.

Sharing great old wines with friends is a lot of fun. Last month my good friend, UK wine writer Matthew Jukes, and I hosted a dinner under the theme of *The History of The Great Australian Red* in conjunction with a wine competition that we were conducting to judge Shiraz Cabernet, Australia's definitive red blend. After spending the day assessing some 166 young wines, we assembled for dinner the great examples of this blend from the last half-century of Australian winemaking. 1962 Penfolds Bin 60A, 1966 Yalumba Galway Vintage Reserve, 1967 Penfolds Bin 7 and 1973 Wolf Blass Black Label set the pace for the night and led into flights of the great Petalumas,

Brokenwoods, Lindemans and Wynns of the '70s, '80s and '90s. Guest speaker, father of the Australian wine industry Len Evans, summed it up: "It is a privilege to taste old Australian wines. Until you taste them it is hard to know just how exquisite they can be."

It is a privilege to taste old Australian wines. Until you taste them it is hard to know just how exquisite they can be
- Len Evans

The extraordinary quality of these wines was preserved by the conditions that they enjoyed in the cellars from which they emerged. These conditions are common to all great cellars. They are the key to unlocking the secrets of great old wines.

stable temperature

A constant temperature is the single most important prerequisite for cellaring wines long-term.

Consider an unfortunate bottle of wine in my friend's kitchen wine rack. On an average day the wine might be stable at, say, 24°C, but in summer, the room may heat up to 30°C. At the same time, the wine in the bottle is likely to warm up to at least 27°C. In doing so, the liquid naturally expands, possibly even pushing the cork out slightly or causing a small amount of wine to be expelled around the cork. (This will quickly evaporate but may leave a slight residue under the capsule.) This movement has also weakened the seal of the cork. When the temperature drops again, the wine cools, contracts and may draw a small amount of air into the bottle around the cork. This can occur even if the wine does not visibly leak past the cork.

Air is the enemy of wine. Prolonged exposure to oxygen causes a wine to age prematurely, ultimately making it flat and lifeless. The colour turns brown, aroma and fruit flavour deteriorate and the wine may become bitter. The wine begins its downhill decline as soon as oxygen enters the bottle. Temperature stability is required in order to avoid this.

While stable temperature is the most important factor in cellaring wine, it can also be one of the most difficult to achieve. This country is hardly renowned for its mild, stable climate! Cellaring wine in most parts of Australia therefore requires some effort to establish a stable temperature. At my home in Brisbane, the annual room temperature varies from around 9°C to 38°C. A bottle of wine stored under these conditions fluctuates from about 14°C to 32°C.

the private cellars of Château Margaux, Bordeaux

Even a 10°C annual variation, as is common in many Australian cellars, is simply too much for reliable long-term cellaring.

The biggest danger, however, is rapid temperature change. Seasonal variations aside, the daily temperature change in our house is often around 10°C. This results in a fluctuation of some 2–3°C in the temperature of a wine bottle every day. This rapid "yo-yo" effect will quickly destroy a wine.

So what is ideal? The smaller the variation, the better. Although it is difficult to pinpoint exact numerical standards, I have achieved excellent results by maintaining a daily bottle temperature variation of less than 0.5°C, a weekly variation of less than 1°C, and a yearly variation of not more than 5°C.

Hugel is one of the most significant wine producers in the Alsace region of north-eastern France. Under its Riquewihr premises, it cellars its Rieslings and Gewürztraminers for up to ten years before release. The temperatures in this cellar vary annually from around 12°C to 14°C. Such fluctuation is quite satisfactory, even for these delicate varieties.

low temperature

Ask the average punter for the most important characteristic of a good cellar and you'll probably hear something about cold temperature. In reality, a low temperature takes second place to a stable temperature on a wine bottle's list of favourite things. Nonetheless, it's an important second place.

The chemical reactions that occur in a wine as it ages are very complex, and not fully understood, but one thing we do know is that their rate depends on the ambient temperature. At high temperatures, say 25°C, these reactions cause the wine to develop very quickly, effectively 'cooking' it. At low temperatures, below 10°C, the wine is virtually frozen into immobility. Somewhere between these extremes lies an ideal compromise, a temperature at which the wine ages slowly and elegantly, but still quickly enough that it will come around within your lifetime. 15°C is a good target, but any constant temperature between about 12°C and 17°C is quite satisfactory.

White wines tend to prefer a slightly lower temperature and sparkling wines even lower again. In the ancient old chalk caverns under Champagne, temperatures are usually between 10°C and 14°C. As one descends to eighteen metres below the surface, the mercury drops to 8°C. Here the greatest of all sparkling wines mature extremely slowly, developing glorious layers of complexity which cannot be replicated by any other wine-producing region on the planet.

The implications of a low storage temperature permeate deeper than just slow, steady development.

In recent months I have found faulty flavours and aromas in two different super-premium wines from two of

Australia's largest and most respected companies. One showed rubbery "reductive" characters, while the other had "horsey" flavours from "brettanomyces" yeast spoilage. Surprised to find these faults in two of my favourite labels, I immediately called the winemakers.

Over the ensuing weeks, after long conversations and bottle after bottle of the same wine from different sources, an interesting and disturbing trend emerged. The bottles of these wines from warmer Queensland warehouses showed faulty reductive or brettanomyces characters, while those from cooler facilities in southern states did not.

The warm conditions had accelerated the onset of these faults over a period of just a few months. These wines are proof that bottles which are quite sound when well-kept can become grossly unstable under warm conditions.

humidity

Once a stable temperature of around 15°C has been achieved, the next thing to address is relative humidity. This requires an insight into how the wine is sealed.

Wines come in a range of different closures these days, with screw caps proving to be the most reliable (see the next chapter for how to look after screw caps in the cellar). Unfortunately, the humble cork is still with us and we must align our cellars to suit its whims. Corks are fussy little creatures. Being a natural substance, they are somewhat prone to deterioration, and won't remain effective for long if they're not looked after. The easiest way to kill a cork is to dry it out, causing it to shrivel, lose its seal, and allow air into the bottle or wine out of the bottle.

128-year-old bottles rest in the walls of Marc Bredif's tenth century rock cellars in the Loire Valley, France

The cork can easily be kept moist on the inside by laying the bottle on its side to maintain contact between the cork and the wine. Keeping the outside from drying out requires a little more attention, and is best achieved by maintaining adequate humidity. Relative humidity around 70–80% is ideal. If the humidity is consistently below 60%, the cork will dry out.

Humidity throughout the ancient cellars of Europe is regularly in the 80–100% range. At Marc Bredif in the Loire Valley in France, the innermost room of the cellar maintains a dead stable temperature of 13°C and a humidity of 90%. Vintages extending right back to 1874 lie perfectly preserved to this day. Well, almost. Bredif has recently constructed a very sterile climate-controlled warehouse to protect its new wines from excess moisture. Humidity above about 85% can cause labels to peel, cartons to rot and bottles to develop mould.

mould grows even on the gate in the cellar of Château de Pommard in Burgundy

Château de Pommard has a different approach in its Burgundy cellars. At 14°C and very high humidity, the mould is apparent even on one-year-old bottles. By the time they are ready for release at ten years of age, a thick jacket makes it difficult to even distinguish one bottle from the next in a stack. But this is of little concern, as they are quickly washed, labelled and dispatched, looking just like new – and, incidentally, also tasting almost just like new. At twelve years of age, the 1989 Château de Pommard was a youthful red-purple with hardly any browning in its colour whatsoever. The fresh raspberry fruit of the palate was more reminiscent of a two-year-old wine than a twelve-year-old. Ideal conditions can make for exceptional longevity.

At home, relabelling a mouldy bottle is not possible, so if you want that prized bottle to look its best when it reaches the dinner table, keep it below 80% humidity. Otherwise the label may emerge at best unattractive, and at worst, unreadable.

darkness

The very best underground cellars are cold, incredibly stable, moist and dank, and of course, very dark. Wines are creatures of the night,

Guigal's cellar in the Rhône is insulated from the vibration of the main road which runs directly over it

emerging from their long hibernation for just one moment of glory. But that moment will be less than glorious if the wine has spent its hibernation on display.

Exposure to light produces chemical reactions in wine that cause it to deteriorate. In particular, ultraviolet light has the greatest effect, and white wines and sparkling wines are the most vulnerable. Amber-coloured bottles provide very good protection, but regrettably these have long since fallen out of fashion to their much less protective clear and green counterparts. The best solution is to keep your cellar in complete darkness whenever it is unattended. Intermittent artificial light will have minimal effect, but daylight should be avoided.

vibration

If you are able to satisfy the demands of the first four conditions for cellaring wines, you are well on your way to enjoying some great old bottles. The last three are of lower consequence, but are worth keeping in mind for the best results. The first of these is avoiding disruption to the wines, both from movement of the bottles and vibration.

Guigal is the most important producer in the famous Côte-Rôtie region of France's Rhône Valley. Outgrowing its 300-year-old cellars in Ampuis, it recently embarked on an enormous construction project. The result is almost two hectares of cellar caverns, climate controlled to 13°C and 80% relative humidity. This proved to be something of an engineering nightmare, with the facility sandwiched between the mighty Rhône River and a train line on one side, and a main road on the other. The finished product not only supports the road, but also Guigal's production facility, with a mass of some five tonnes per square metre!

Traffic rumbling across the top of the cellar is detrimental to the development of Guigal's wines. As wines mature, larger and more complex molecules are produced that eventually fall out of the solution as sediment. Under stable conditions, these settle along the bottom of the bottle or barrel, allowing the wine to develop fully. Movement disrupts this process, stirring the sediment and mixing it throughout the wine.

The solution at Guigal was to construct an advanced anti-vibration system throughout the entire cellar structure. While most of us do not have problems of such a scale at home, vibration can still pose a threat. Mechanical cooling units are prime culprits.

Further to this problem, there are extreme phenomena such as 'travel shock', after extended transportation. It may take weeks or even months to settle before it is again at its best. Closely related is 'bottle shock', where the wine takes some time to recover from the bottling process.

ventilation

Ventilation can be damaging to wines because it can upset the delicate temperature balance in the cellar. While gentle air currents in themselves are of little consequence, the danger arises when these currents influence the temperature in all or part of the cellar. In particular, artificial cooling units have a tendency to introduce cold air currents.

There needs to be something of a compromise here. While moving air is often a necessity in maintaining a stable temperature throughout the cellar, the air should not be of such a temperature, or moved so quickly, as to cause rapid fluctuations in bottle temperature. Where absolute perfection cannot be attained, it is sufficient to ensure that stiff breezes directed at the bottles are avoided, particularly if they have the potential to change the bottle temperature.

odour

Corks are semi-permeable and it is possible for intense odours in the cellar to permeate the wine. For this reason, an ideal cellar should be free of odours. Your cellar may well be the perfect temperature and humidity to mature your beloved hunk of stinky blue cheese, but for the sake of your wines, keep it well clear!

These seven steps are the key to enjoying great old wine. The difference that they make will blow your mind. The conclusion to my friend's 389 story was that I took him a bottle from my own cellar – exactly the same wine purchased from the same place on the same day, seven years earlier. The comparison was like night and day – it was fruity, structured and had at least a decade of life still left in it.

He's building a cellar now.

screw your cellar

Last month I tipped a $190 bottle of prestige Champagne down the sink. It was a beautiful fancy bottle in one of those posh presentation boxes with a ribbon around it. I pulled the cork and poured the wine and knew straight away that something was wrong. It tasted dusty, like mouldy wet cardboard. My Champagne was 'corked' – ruined by a taint that haphazardly affects natural corks, irreversibly destroying the wine. It went straight down the sink. All $190 of it. That's why I don't like corks.

I had opportunity to visit Tokyo on a couple of occasions last year to host a series of seminars with Wine Australia for the Japanese wine trade. The topic was screw caps, and we assembled a line up of older wines under both cork and screw cap to demonstrate how wine ages under the two closures.

The most memorable wine of the tasting was a screw-capped bottle of 1980 Yalumba Pewsey Vale Riesling. Sourced directly from Yalumba's museum cellar in the depths of its historic Angaston headquarters, this twenty-five-year-old wine was in remarkable condition. The colour was a vibrant, glowing yellow, with not a hint of the characteristic browning that so often characterises the downward decline of older whites. The flavour was every bit as outstanding as the colour – toasty, marmalade, lemon butter, honeysuckle and spice welled up into a crescendo of complexity over a backbone of fine, soft, dancing acidity which lingered long into the aftertaste. This phenomenal wine still had a decade of life left in it. It was singularly the best old Riesling that I have tasted in my life. But then, there never was any question that white wines can age magnificently under screw cap.

The question of bottling age-worthy red wines under screw cap has been long-debated. Again, the most convincing evidence is in the glass. Penfolds provided three bottles of Bin 389 Cabernet Sauvignon Shiraz 1996 for our tasting in Japan. The first two were sealed with corks, both had dusty, corky wood flavours and in one case, the fruit was flat and lifeless – the variabilities of cork. The third bottle was screw-capped, from a trial commenced by Penfolds a decade ago. It showed spicier fruit characters than the first two, with more pronounced plum, dark berry and chocolate/coffee flavours. The

1996 Penfolds Bin 389 and 1980 Pewsey Vale

wine was better balanced, with fine tannins and red cherry acidity supporting a memorable finish. It only left me disappointed that I couldn't buy it under screw cap for my own cellar!

Evidence such as this has given winemakers all over the world confidence to bottle their age-worthy red wines under screw cap. Many great old screw-capped reds have been opened in recent years, including 1964 and 1966 Burgundy, 1983 Yalumba Claret and 1995 Irvine Grand Merlot (see the books on page 8 for further detail).

Not only do these wines age well under screw cap, they age better than the same wines under cork. Screw caps provide a more reliable seal, allowing less air to pass through than the average cork, thus eliminating the damaging effects of contact with oxygen. French winemaker Michel Laroche commented to me recently, "Now, when a friend asks me if he should take his wine in screw cap, I say, 'If it's a wine that's not going to age for long, it doesn't matter, provided you accept that a certain proportion will be tainted. But if you really buy serious bottles of wine that you want to age for years, please take them in screw cap!'"

Why such confidence? As screw caps continue to take off, their implications become all the more apparent. And there is no place where this is more pronounced than in the conditions required for ideal cellaring.

Corks are difficult little creatures to keep happy. Of all of the conditions required for an ideal cellar, something like half of them are only there to please the cork. Do away with the cork and all of a sudden establishing a perfect cellar is not nearly such a daunting proposition. In taking on screw caps we are able to rewrite the rules of wine cellaring.

If you really buy serious bottles of wine that you want to age for years, please take them in screw cap! **- Michel Laroche**

---

stable temperature

The most important - and most difficult - pre-requisite for ideal cellaring is a stable temperature. Fluctuating temperatures cause wines to expand and contract, producing pressure changes inside the bottle that threaten the integrity of the seal. Research indicates that screw caps can withstand pressure changes in excess of four times those that corks can handle. This means that when the temperature rises and the cork moves, the screw cap stays rock solid. Screw caps hold their seal more reliably than corks under extreme conditions.

This ability of screw caps to protect wine against temperature fluctuations has a direct and verifiable impact on the quality of the wine. David Leyland of bottle manufacturer ACI in Melbourne is in a unique position to attest to this. His collection of wines, remnants from screw cap trials during the 1970s, must have been one of the only collections in existence that contained the same old wines sealed under both cork and screw cap and stored under less than ideal conditions. He finished drinking the last of them recently and told me that all of the corked samples were oxidised to the point of being undrinkable, while the screw-capped wines were, "pretty good, still drinkable with no sign of oxidation."

low temperature

While a stable temperature is not as significant for screw-capped wines as it is for their corked counterparts, a low temperature is still crucial. In the ACI Stelvin Trial during the 1970s, bottles were divided into two groups, one stored in a specially built cellar maintained within one degree of thirteen degrees Celsius, the other at 'Melbourne ambient,' within two degrees of twenty-two degrees Celsius. A report on the trial concluded that "the closures overall gave better results at the lower temperatures of storage. The influence of the closure comparisons are generally greater at the higher storage temperatures." More recent trials performed by the Australian Wine Research Institute have drawn similar conclusions.

Despite the superior temperature-handling capabilities of screw caps, it should be noted that wine can be damaged by high temperatures

an eight-year Riesling vertical testifies to the consistent manner in which wine develops under screw cap even if the cap retains its seal. Temperatures above 20°C will cause wine to develop prematurely, while temperatures above 30°C should be avoided under all circumstances. Particular care should be taken during the transportation of wine. It is possible for temperatures in a parked car to rise above 80°C. Warehouses and trucks also tend to heat up to dangerous levels.

humidity

Humidity in the cellar is the area in which screw caps afford the greatest advantage. With corks, this is at best a delicately balanced compromise. To keep the corks from drying out and the wines from evaporating, humidity must be as high as possible. To avoid mould and peeling labels it should be as low as possible. While 75 percent appears to keep both sides happy, in reality even this level can still present problems in either direction.

With screw caps, there is absolutely no need to maintain sufficient humidity in order to sustain the seal. Keep it low to keep the labels happy. Further, there is no requirement to store bottles horizontally. The only reason for doing so with cork-sealed bottles is to keep the inside of the cork moist and hence reduce the likelihood of cork failure and consequent oxygen ingress. This can have its disadvantages, such as the need to stand old red wines upright for a few days to allow sediment to settle before decanting. Penfolds chief winemaker Peter Gago adds, "When opening wines under screw cap there is no need to worry about tasting them before serving, regardless of whether they've been stored upright or horizontally."

That said, there is one advantage in cellaring screw-capped bottles horizontally. A recent temporary malfunction in a glass factory in France resulted in a small number of leaking bottles. A few Australian wine producers were affected, and immediately replaced any returned bottles. The advantage of storing bottles horizontally is that it allows any damage to the cap or the seal to be easily detected through visible leakage.

odour

The final advantage of screw caps in the cellar is a further consequence of their air-tight seal. Screw caps are impermeable to odours that may taint the wine. Cellar odours, potentially damaging to corked bottles, present no hazard for screw-capped wines.

While the conditions for cellaring with screw caps are not particularly difficult to establish, there is one way in which they must be cared for which is not so obvious.

dented caps

The screw cap liner provides a reliable seal against oxygen and other gases over many years, provided there is no external damage to the cap. The strength of the seal at the top of the bottle is less hard-wearing than it is for cork bottles, and as such, screw caps require a greater degree of protection from damage. If the edge of the cap is given a sharp knock, the seal may be broken. The new screw cap specification diminishes this risk substantially, through a closer fit between the cap and the top edge of the bottle. However, there is still potential for the seal to be damaged if the screw cap is knocked against another bottle or hard surface.

further developments

The implications of the impact of screw caps on home cellaring are significant. But the advantages may extend further than we are aware. The effects of a less-than-ideal cellaring environment are exaggerated in smaller-format bottles, where the cork-to-wine ratio is large. Fluctuating cellar temperatures can draw air in around the cork and cause oxidation of the wine. Hence, smaller bottles may experience greater oxygen ingress and are generally inferior in the long-term. The reverse is true for large format bottles such as magnums, which are regarded as longer-lived, for no other reason than that relatively less oxygen is able to enter the bottle and develop the wine. Consequently, a magnum is said to facilitate better development of the wine throughout its life.

In the case of screw-capped wines, where oxygen ingress is virtually eliminated, this prompts some interesting questions. Will wines sealed with screw caps develop in the same way regardless of bottle size? And will these wines invariably develop better than their corked counterparts? The evidence to date suggests that the answer to both questions may well be, "yes." The future will tell.

Screw caps are the cellar's best friend.

What is clear for now is that screw caps are the cellar's best friend because they resist temperature and pressure changes, they are completely unperturbed by humidity, impermeable to odour and can be stored upright.

The message is simple: make sure your cellar is screwed.

Yalumba Pewsey Vale Riesling 1976 was Australia's first commercial screw-capped wine

stock your cellar

The most important part of your cellar is what goes into it and when you pull it out. This is where you can have the most fun!

Keep your mind open to learning. Ask your favourite bottle shop salesperson, check out the latest wine column and grab a copy of my annual wine guide, *Taste Food & Wine*. Most of all, learn by tasting. Try different wines whenever you can, order something you've never tried before and get along to the free tastings at your local bottle shop. Buy a case of wine and try a bottle every six months to see how it develops. Then drink the rest when you like it best, keeping one bottle for later to see where it's going.

how to pick a white for the cellar

Any wine cellar devoted only to red wines is missing half the fun.

Acidity is the lifeblood of all white wines in the cellar. You can detect acidity as a sourness on the palate and a sharpness on the sides of the tongue – like sucking a lemon. At the most basic level, if a white wine has lots of acidity it may age well, if it doesn't, it certainly won't.

The two great Australian whites with the acidity to go the distance are Riesling and Semillon. Relinquishing the racy acidity and zesty citrus flavours of their youth, these varieties take on rich complexity of toast, honey and dried fruits as they mature. Look for Semillons from the Hunter Valley in New South Wales and Rieslings from South Australia's Clare and Eden Valleys, Western Australia's Frankland River and Victoria's Henty.

Riesling and Semillon possess the talent of drinking well in their youth and in their maturity, but not always in between. They commonly go through something of a "hole" in their development, a time during which the freshness of youth clashes with the complexity of maturity, leaving the wine tasting awkward and unappealing for some years. As a general guide, drink a premium Australian Riesling or Semillon in its first few years or between five and ten years of age. The best will live for many decades under a screw cap in an ideal cellar.

Australian Chardonnay can be something of an enigma when it comes to the cellar. Most are best in their extreme youth. If a wine needs some time for the influence of oak to integrate with its fruit flavours, provided that it has the tight acidity to last the distance, my general rule is to drink it within five years of vintage. I have found only a handful of Australian Chardonnays which improve much beyond this time. They tend to be lean, cool climate styles at the more expensive end of town. Tyrrell's Vat 47 is a notable example.

Most other Australian white wines are at their prime while they are still young and fresh. Sauvignon Blanc should always be drunk in the twelve months following vintage (of course, there will always be a one-

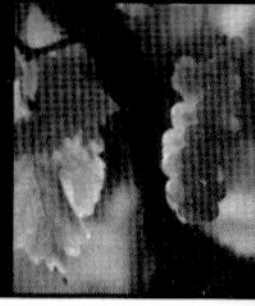

in-a-thousand exception, but I'll leave it to you to discover it). Verdelho, Viognier, Gewürztraminer, Pinot Gris and the whole gamut of other soft, fruity styles have little to gain from time in solitary confinement. The exceptions will be lean, tightly-structured acidic examples from cool climate regions. Marsanne and Roussanne and blends of the two can produce long-lived wines if they are not too oily or heavy.

The same rules apply to dessert wines, with acidity again the key and Riesling and Semillon leading the way on the cellar front. Australian stickies are best in the first decade of their life, although the greatest of the sweet wines of Sauternes in France will easily outlive you and me.

whites for the cellar

Riesling	Marsanne
Semillon	Roussanne
Chardonnay	Dessert wines

how to pick a red for the cellar

If acidity is the lifeblood of a white wine in the cellar, the powerhouse of a red is tannin. Tannin is the astringent character that gives a drying, sandpaper-like feel on the inside of your cheeks. It comes from grape skins, seeds and stalks as well as the wood in oak barrels. Chew on a grape seed sometime and you'll discover tannin!

As a red wine develops in the cellar it "feeds" off its tannins. The wine softens as the tannins slowly fall out of solution to become sediment. As with white wines, an ideal red for the cellar will show good fruit flavours and appropriate levels of acidity.

The bottom line is balance, and this is the singular most important characteristic of all great wines. Look for appropriate levels of fruit, oak, tannin, acid and alcohol. If one or more of these stick out inappropriately when the wine is young, it will never rectify itself in the cellar. While age will never 'fix' a bad wine, it will give a great wine wings to fly higher.

Cabernet Sauvignon is the king of the cellar. The most age-worthy wine in the world tends to begin its life as an astringent, dark, blackcurrant-flavoured heavyweight, but as it ages, it tones and softens to take on flavours like tobacco and capsicum. Its hallowed turf in Australia is in Western Australia's Margaret River and South Australia's Coonawarra, and these wines should form a cornerstone of your cellar. It also performs quite well in Geographe, Great Southern, Central Victoria, some higher altitude areas in New South Wales and virtually everywhere in South Australia. I have enjoyed Australian Cabernets at ten, twenty, thirty and more years of age (the wines, that is, not me!).

Merlot, Cabernet Franc, Petit Verdot and Malbec all cellar well on their own, but best serve as subjects of the noble Cabernet Sauvignon, with which they are often blended. The best of the wines of Bordeaux, the birthplace of this blend, will easily live for fifty or more years.

Cabernet Shiraz blends are a cellaring specialty. The great Australian red blend is alive and well in wine regions across South Australia, Victoria, New South Wales and Western Australia. The very best of these blends have the patience to live for half a century in the cellar (assuming you have the patience to wait for them!).

Shiraz is Australia's most famous red, and it deserves a large section in your cellar. The most versatile red grape in the country morphs itself from big, inky-black creations in South Australia's Barossa Valley and McLaren Vale to highly-toned black pepper, herb and spice incarnations in the cooler reaches of Victoria, and it hardly misses any region or style in between. The good news is that it is eminently age-worthy at both ends of the spectrum, and as it develops it converges toward a more earthy, chocolatey, mellow style. Twenty years is a breeze for top-shelf Aussie Shiraz.

Grenache is the trusty side-kick of Shiraz, and the best examples of its delightful three-way partnership with Mourvèdre will happily evolve to ever-higher planes of earthy, spicy complexity over many years. On its own, the juicy, fruity appeal of Grenache is best exploited in its youth, but the Barossa Valley and McLaren Vale produce a number of top examples that will easily see out a decade.

Pinot Noir is eminently more age-worthy in its spiritual home of Burgundy than on our shores, but don't let this stop you from laying down a great example from Victoria, Tassie, New Zealand or the coolest parts of South Australia for up to a decade. Only if you have the will-power to do so, of course. I don't, so these wines are lucky if they last for more than five years in my cellar!

Nebbiolo is a grape that can be so tough in its youth that it positively demands time in the cellar to settle to a more amenable composure. More at home in Italy, a few examples are now popping up in Australia, and they're worth popping into your cellar for a good deal of time.

I could go on for many pages and still not cover all of the red grapes planted in this country. The only other examples that deserve a brief moment of your attention, if only to increase the diversity in your cellar, are Durif and Zinfandel (long-term) and Sangiovese and Tempranillo (medium-term).

reds for the cellar

Cabernet Sauvignon	Grenache
Merlot	Pinot Noir
Cabernet Franc	Nebbiolo
Petit Verdot	Durif
Malbec	Zinfandel
Shiraz	Sangiovese
Mourvèdre	Tempranillo

how to pick a sparkling wine for the cellar

Sparkling wines from cool regions like Tasmania, Southern Victoria and high altitude areas in Victoria and New South Wales can age extremely well. In general, non-vintage (NV) wines are intended to be consumed on release, while a particularly crisp, tight, vintage wine may age for up to a decade.

Great old Champagne is one of the loves of my life, and there is little that I adore more than a great vintage wine with a couple of decades behind it. Again, drink the NVs on release, stick the very best vintages in the cellar, and be as patient as you can be.

This is an opportune time to slot in a plug for sparkling red, Australia's own specialty wine style. Most often based on Shiraz, I have also found great examples made from Merlot, Cabernet and blends of the three. As with sparkling whites, the carbon dioxide trapped in the wine discourages the deteriorating influence of oxygen, allowing the youthful glory of the wine to be sustained for decades longer than it would otherwise be. I have recently tasted Seppelt Show Sparkling Shiraz from six different decades, and every bottle was glorious. The 1953 still had bubbles fifty years later!

sparkling wines for the cellar

Vintage whites and rosés
Vintage Champagne
Sparkling reds

how to pick a fortified wine for the cellar

We've already tossed around sweeties under whites above, but fortified wines deserve a mention of their own, because confusion is rife in this area.

The great Muscats and Tokays of Rutherglen and tawny-style (previously called Port) wines of the Barossa Valley and Central Victoria are created as a blend of many vintages aged for decades in old barrels. These wines are painstakingly assembled to balance the complexity of this old material with the freshness of younger parcels. They are not going to get any better once they are in bottle.

The exceptions in Australia's fortifieds are the VP wines (previously called Vintage Port). Created from a single vintage, these wines are a lay-down misère in the cellar. They demand age to soften and will blossom to hitherto unknown delights after twenty years. Perpetually out of fashion, in recent

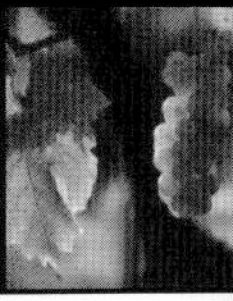

years I've picked up epic examples from the 1980s at auction for under $25. Real Vintage Ports (from Portugal, of course will set you back a little more both in cost and in time in the cellar.

fortified wines for the cellar

Australian VPs
Vintage Port

when to drink it

Every year I review some five thousand wine for my columns, articles and books, and one of my tasks in this process is to ascribe every wine a "drinking window," a time frame over which I expect it to be at its prime. This can be something of a black art, since some of my readers will enjoy the vibrancy of youth while others prefer the mellow complexity of old age. To accommodate this spectrum of tastes, a drinking window is usually a range rather than a single year, and it wouldn't be a bad approach for you to adopt a similar system. Give every wine in your cellar a drinking range, and taste different bottles over this time, finishing the rest when you like it best.

There are no easy rules for working out when this might be, but it's a fun process to find out by tasting wines at different ages to build up a knowledge of how they develop and when you are most likely to enjoy them. As a simple starting point, provided the wine is balanced, the more acidic a white wine and the more tannic a red wine, the more likely it is to age well.

There will be some wines in your cellar that don't develop in the way that you'd hoped. It pays to go through your cellar every few years and put these aside. Maybe they will appeal to someone else's taste, so offer them to a friend who likes that style or send them to auction. Invest the proceeds in wines that you enjoy.

Selecting wines for your cellar and discovering how they improve is an exciting and addictive process. At every step, keep an open mind and think laterally about your drinking needs in two, five and ten years' time. Try wine styles that you've never explored before – you never know what might be your favourite thing in five years, but if your cellar selection is diverse now, you'll be well prepared with a few bottles to surprise yourself when the time comes.

good enough

Your senses might be deceiving you. I have a friend with a cellar under his house on the Gold Coast. The house is on a steep hill, with the cellar cut into the hillside such that most of it lies underground. The walls are Besser brick and the exposed side is well protected from the elements by a dense garden. He described it to me as the perfect cellar: moist, cool in summer and warm in winter. But ultimately the thermometer was the true judge. With a winter minimum of 13°C and a summer maximum of 27°C, the wine in his bottles was experiencing at least 10°C of annual variation. The first rule of assessing cellar suitability is that subjective judgements can be misleading.

My cellar holds its temperature to within a degree of 15°C. When I open it in summer I am confronted by a mass of cold air. It feels like a refrigerator. When I first opened it in winter I got an unpleasant shock. It was warm in there! After a momentary panic, I checked the thermometer and was relieved to find that it was still dead on 15°C. Good pilots rely on their instruments, not their perceptions. There's a lesson in this.

cellar monitoring instruments

The most important instrument for monitoring a cellar is a thermometer with the capacity to record maximum and minimum temperatures. Two types are available: the traditional double-bulb thermometer, and more recently, the digital thermometer. The latter is available from good hardware shops, department stores and electronics outlets everywhere. I found an Acme model for $7 in Woolworths once. It records the current, maximum and minimum temperatures, both outside and inside, to an accuracy of 0.5°C. I prefer a more up-market model from Dick Smith Electronics in the form of a *TempTec Hygrometer and In/Out Thermometer*. For $50 it contains all of the features of the Coyote model, but with accuracy to 0.1°C, plus a hygrometer with minimum and maximum memory to monitor humidity. There are plenty of variations on the market to suit your preferences and budget.

tech tip

build a bottle thermometer

If you are prepared to go to a little extra trouble, a few small modifications convert the *TempTec* unit into a useful bottle thermometer.

The "inside" humidity and temperature probes are located inside the casing, while the "outside" probe is connected to the unit by a long wire. In order to observe your cellar conditions from outside, it would be more useful if all of the probes were outside of the casing. Relocating the two probes is not a difficult task if you have an ounce of skill in wielding a soldering iron. It's also quite safe.

Unscrew the back panel from the unit and unscrew the circuit board at the bottom. Turn it over and look for the probes soldered to the board. The temperature probe is the little round blue one and the humidity probe is the rectangular white one. Desolder them from the board, being careful not to overheat the temperature probe (I use pointy nosed pliers to hold the legs of the probe and to act as a heatsink). Solder the ends of a two-core cable to the points where the probes were located. Fine speaker wire does the trick nicely. Now punch a hole in a screw cap from a wine bottle, poke the wire through and solder the other ends of the cables to the two probes. Where the cables exit the device, cut the hole slightly larger to accommodate the new wires.

Now waterproof the temperature probe. A small waterproof tube such as a biro casing sealed with super glue would be effective.

Seal the cable to the screw cap to create a water-tight seal using a strong adhesive like super glue. Fill a wine bottle with water, insert the probe and screw it on tight. Before the days of screw caps, I did this with corks instead, and the bottle would invariably leak. Ah, the joys of corks!

Desolder the humidity probe from inside the casing and connect it to the end of another pair of wires, in the same manner as the temperature probe. This device will now monitor the air temperature, bottle temperature and humidity in your cellar.

Warning: *Do not carry your bottle thermometer in your hand luggage on International flights. (Not a good look!)*

a digital thermometer can be quickly transformed into a handy bottle thermometer

cellaring locations

Armed with your new contraption, you can now check out some prime cellaring locations in your home. A good start is an inside room without any exterior walls that heat up in the sun. A linen cupboard in such a room is even better. A little extra protection can be provided by leaving wines in their cases, or even wrapping bottles in newspaper. In any case, bottles sealed with natural cork should be cellared horizontally to ensure that the cork stays moist. Remember that in any location, it is the extremes of temperature that are most telling, so be sure to note summer maximums and winter minimums.

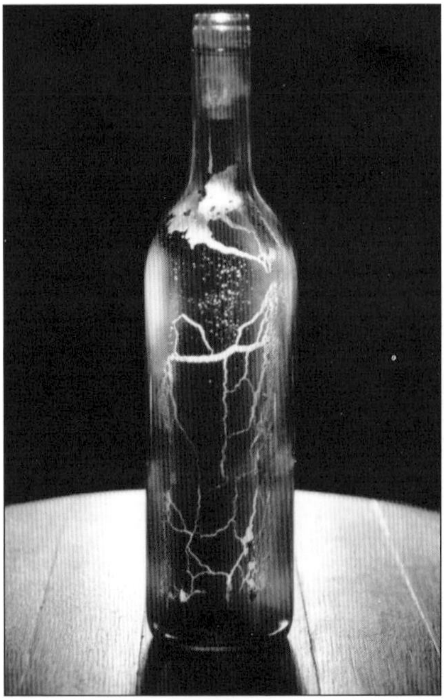

Underground cellars are a romantic option, but may prove to be a lot of trouble for little gain. In many parts of Australia, even the ground temperature varies by 10°C annually. If you're going to need just as much insulation or artificial cooling underground, save the expense of digging and spend it on wine instead.

If you find a location in your home to be satisfactory according to the conditions outlined on pages 16 through 22, pour yourself a big glass of something decadent, sit back and relax. You're a lucky sod, and you probably live in a remote outpost on the southern coast of Tasmania (cheers!). For the rest of us, a little more effort is required.

many red wines "throw a crust" by depositing sediment as they mature

where do I start?

So you've got a few dozen bottles stashed away. Now, let's be realistic. Are you cellaring them for the long-term or simply storing them to drink soon? In my house, they wouldn't have a hope of lasting a few months, let alone a few years. There's nothing wrong with this, but you're not talking about cellaring .

The good news for you is that your wine storage needs are very simple. You don't need an elaborate cellar. There are only two rules for you to remember: Take a white wine out of the fridge a little while before you serve it, and put a red wine in the fridge a little while before your serve it. This way you won't be drinking your whites too cold or your reds too warm. In other words, forget about cellaring and get on with drinking. Cheers, and pour me a glass while you're at it!

If you live in a warm place or have a bottle or two that sit around for a year or more, storage conditions will really start to take their toll. The first foe to overcome is also the most deadly: daily temperature variation. It is rapid temperature fluctuation that most quickly deteriorates wine. The single most effective weapon against this is insulation.

While cardboard boxes and newspaper provide some insulation, there is a better alternative that is equally inexpensive. Supermarkets and greengrocers regularly have an oversupply of polystyrene broccoli boxes, and many are happy to give these away. The most I've ever been charged is a few dollars. These boxes come with airtight lids and are easily stacked. (You can also purchase professional polystyrene wine boxes, but the lids don't tend to fit if the bottles are slightly oversized, and they'll set you back $60 for a dozen box.) The broccoli boxes are the perfect size to house 18 bottles of various sizes and shapes and still allow room for layers of newspaper to provide further insulation. By storing wines close together in this way, the effect of 'safety in numbers' also promotes temperature stability and minimises rapid fluctuations.

In a cool location over a period of six months I have found that the

a polystyrene broccoli box makes a great first cellar

daily temperature variation of the air in the boxes never exceeds 1°C, while the weekly variation is always less than 2°C. The temperature variation inside the bottles tends to be slightly less again. This is a significant improvement over the 10°C fluctuation in the air temperature in the room. However, this system does little to combat seasonal temperature variation, with the boxes as low as 15°C in mid-winter and as high as 28.5°C at the height of summer. Nonetheless, the elimination of rapid temperature variation is certainly a helpful first step.

not permanent - thank goodness - only in transit!

But is this good enough? For a few dozen bottles with a life expectancy of a year or two, simple inexpensive solutions such as polystyrene boxes are probably quite adequate. Incidentally, you wouldn't want to stash hundreds of bottles in this way because accessing bottles in the bottom box - and indeed the bottom bottle in any box - is a dickens of a job. When your collection grows, you'll quickly tire of the inconvenience of this system.

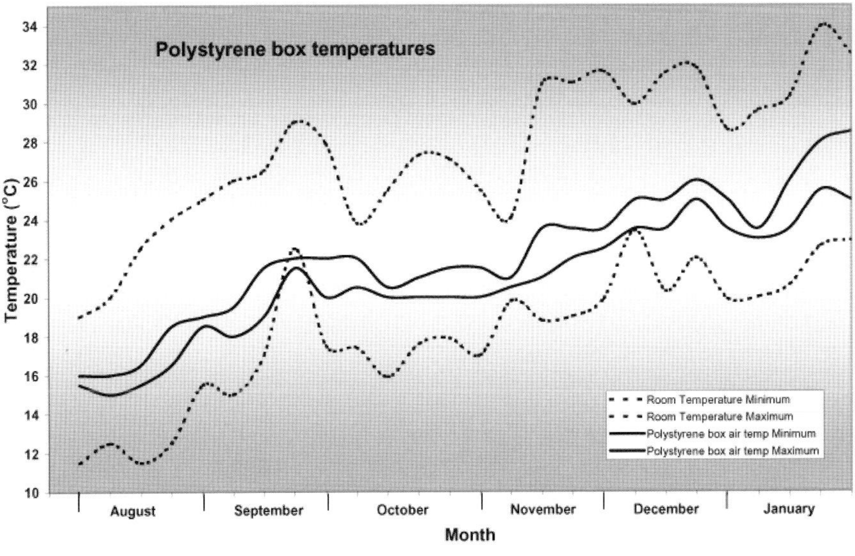

My father-in-law's cellar is located under a stairwell in the centre of his house. The area was conveniently walled-off when the house was built, with large cupboard doors installed to allow access. While the space was perfect, the temperature was not. Not wanting to go to too much expense, he opted for a simple insulating system. I donated some sheets of 5cm thick polystyrene that were left over from some of my own cellar projects. After lining the walls, doors and the underside of the stairs above, the temperature stability of the space was improved considerably.

In recent years a new option has emerged for storing a few dozen bottles. It seems that the latest kitchen fashion statement is a wine "fridge" and units the size of a small bar fridge often come up on special at department stores for around $200. They're not particularly well-suited for long-term cellaring, but the life-expectancy of your few dozen bottles was never that high, anyway. These things are great for keeping your current drinking stock within easy reach. The added bonus is that they keep your wines close to the right drinking temperature – just give whites a brief spell in the fridge and reds a brief spell on the counter and they'll be spot on. I love this feature as I'm always grabbing a bottle at the last minute, and desperately trying to get it to the right temperature as quickly as possible!

decant it

Always decant a full-bodied red wine from the cellar before you serve it. Decanting involves pouring the wine from the bottle to another container. Many red wines deposit sediment in the bottle ("throw a crust") as they mature. Decanting serves the dual purpose of leaving the sediment behind and allowing the wine to "open up" through contact with air. There are all sorts of exotic decanters available, but any glass jug will do the trick. To decant a red, stand it upright for a day to allow the sediment to settle, open it carefully without shaking it up and then pour it into the decanter slowly and evenly. Look through the neck of the bottle to watch the flow of the wine and stop pouring as soon as you see sediment creeping near the neck. Looking through the neck at a candle can help with this process, but any light will work (a friend puts a Dolphin torch to good use for his best bottles!). You can then pour from the decanter, or double-decant back into the bottle (after rinsing the sediment out of the bottle). The older the wine, the shorter the time it should spend in the decanter.

raid the fridge

Some wines undergo miraculous transformations in the cellar. A vertical tasting of Tahbilk Marsanne was one of the most revealing experiences that I have had with the changes that occur in white wine as it ages. Some Australian wineries hold back vintages of their classic wines for release as mature bottles, and this can be an exciting way to discover the styles of wine that are worth cellaring (without the wait!). A few years ago, Tahbilk offered vintages of its classic white Marsanne from the past twelve years, so I quickly assembled a group of friends and we tasted our way from 1998 back to 1988.

The contrast was phenomenal. The 1998 was a fresh, light wine, very pale yellow with a tint of green in colour and displaying an intense variety of tropical, lime and gooseberry fruit flavours. The 1988 was verging on golden orange and was incredibly intense, very smooth and soft. Its flavours resembled rich butterscotch, honey and camphor wood. The same wine from the same place made by the same person, but a decade of difference made it hard to believe that they were the same thing. The magic of the cellar is truly captivating, but it must be nurtured carefully if it is to work its spell.

The biggest evil to permeate a cellar and slowly destroy bottles is temperature variation. While white wines are most sensitive to this deterioration, all wines require a stable environment in order to mature to their potential. The good news is that it doesn't necessarily take expensive technological weapons to tackle this problem.

When your collection grows to around 10 dozen bottles, it's time to make sure that you can house them under the right conditions, because some of these bottles are going to hang around for the long-term. This is where commercial wine cabinets come into their own. For between about $3 000 and $20 000 you can invest in a professional cabinet that is custom-built to provide just the right conditions for long-term wine cellaring. Some models also come in a multi-zone format, in which different sections hold different

a professional wine cabinet such as this Transtherm Loft is a reliable way to cellar wine temperatures to keep every bottle at its ideal serving temperature.

Units like these are impressive pieces of furniture for a hip kitchen, but if you're happy to go for a retro feel, you can put something together yourself at a fraction of the cost. The weekly 'For Sale' column of any newspaper is lined with devices that can be transformed into some of the simplest and most economical climate-controlled cellars of all – the humble refrigerator.

I've now gone through three refrigerators as cellars, and I've paid between $20 and $100 for each of them. The first one simply served as a big insulated cupboard. A 350L Kelvinator fridge 'only' held 120 bottles, and when it wasn't running, the air temperature inside the fridge varied by around 1°C to 2°C every week and 10°C over a year. These results were similar to those of my polystyrene broccoli boxes. A slight odour was eliminated by placing an open container of bicarbonate of soda inside the unit.

There are a few things to look for in an old fridge for wine storage. First, the classic metal grille shelves can handle the weight of a number of rows of bottles much better than the modern flimsy plastic shelves. Secondly, avoid frost-free units if you can, as running the cooling system will dehumidify the air and dry out the corks. A 'fridge only' (no freezer) avoids the frost-free issue and provides greater storage capacity as well as eliminating the 'super-chilled' freezer section. A friend with a freezer section experiences problems with condensed moisture every time the refrigerator completes its regular cycle. In addition to these design characteristics, the condition of the unit is also important. The state of the door seals is particularly significant, as these have a large bearing on the effectiveness of the insulation. The seals should be soft and make a tight seal around the entire door. If this is not the case, they can be replaced, but at a cost.

a humble old fridge can become an effective cellar

checklist for the ideal wine fridge

Metal grille shelves

Not frost-free

Fridge only

Door seals in good condition

Refrigerators such as these can be quite effective for short-term wine storage. They offer an advantage of accessibility that broccoli boxes do not. By numbering shelves and recording bottle locations in a cellar record (see an example at the end of this book), bottles can be located and removed quickly and with minimal disruption of other bottles. The reduction in weekly temperature variation is pleasing, although the annual temperature range is still a concern. During a particularly hot summer week, the temperature in my fridge hit 25°C. A friend with a similar unit in his garage reported a disastrous 32°C. Conditions such as these demand climate control.

thermostat

The thermostat is the device that sets and controls the temperature in a refrigerator. Standard refrigerator thermostats are inadequate for cellaring wine on two counts. The first is simply that they are rarely able to be adjusted above about 8–10°C (a bit too chilly for our bottled friends). The second problem is less obvious but more important. The 'temperature differential' of a thermostat is the difference between the temperature at which it turns on and the temperature at which it turns off. The thermostat turns on the cooling unit when the temperature rises, and off when it falls. For instance, a thermostat that turns on at 6°C and off at 2°C would have a 4°C differential. Such a differential is typical for many refrigeration thermostats, but it introduces a problem in our wine cellar. If the air temperature varies by 4°C every time the cooling system comes on, the bottle temperature will vary frequently, and we undo the main purpose of cooling altogether. Remember that a stable temperature is more important than a low temperature.

tech tip **install a new thermostat**

Wine cellars require a thermostat with a small differential. A good option is a 'Capillary thermostat' from RS Components. It is variable between -30°C and +35°C and has a differential of 1.5°C, small enough for the air cycle not to vary the bottle temperature. Look up stock number 250-6061 at www.rs-components.com.au and expect to pay about $40. You'll need to get a qualified electrician to complete the thermostat exchange for you. This is a simple job and shouldn't cost too much, particularly if you are able to mount the new thermostat yourself and just leave the wiring to him or her. A plastic 'jiffy' box from electronics suppliers like Dick Smith Electronics is a good way to house the unit. While the capillary system allows the thermostat control to be placed outside of the cellar environment, this is not recommended. While the units are supposed to rely only on the temperature of the capillary probe itself, the temperature of the control unit seems to influence its performance very slightly.

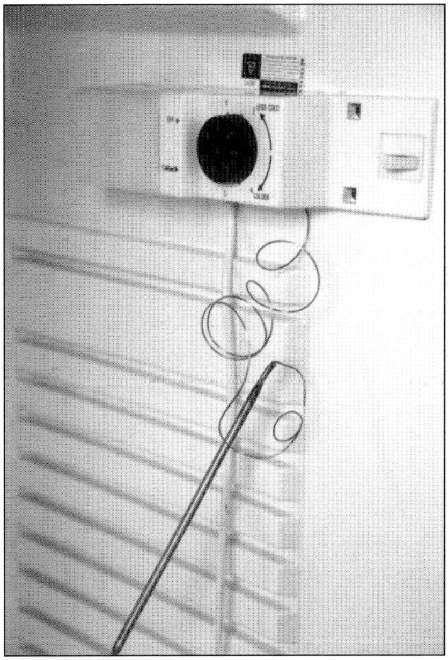

Placement of the thermostat probe about two-thirds of the way up the cabinet seems to be ideal. There is something of a compromise involved here. If the thermostat is directly in the air flow close to the

conversion of a fridge involves installation of a new thermostat (below and right), a fan for air flow (below right) and a bucket and towel system for humidity (see page 66)

cooling unit, it may cause the cycle to be very rapid, with the unit turning on and off too regularly. On the other hand, if the thermostat is too far out of the air flow, a slow cycle will cause the bottle temperature to rise and fall slightly during each cycle. Using your bottle temperature thermometer (page 36), experiment with different placements of the thermostat probe to get the cycle time as long as possible without the bottle temperature changing noticeably.

tech tip — **install a timer**

Adding a new thermostat to a refrigerator might be more trouble and expense than you're up for. A simpler solution for reducing seasonal variation is to run the unit intermittently during the warmer months of the year. You can pick up an electrical timer from hardware and department stores for as little as a few dollars and plug it in without any rewiring. Set the timing such that it cuts in for quarter-hour bursts during the warmest part of the day. Experiment with the timing and you should be able to 'chop off' the summer maximum temperatures by at least a few degrees.

A good alternative to the capillary thermostat is a digital unit. These are available from commercial refrigeration suppliers and offer a few advantages over the standard analogue devices. First, the temperature is entered exactly, rather than simply rotating a dial and hoping that it's right. Secondly, and more significantly, digital thermostats also allow the differential to be adjusted. This can eliminate some of the experimentation with placement that is necessary with other thermostats. These devices also provide exact temperature readouts and detailed programming and control facilities (but at a price).

an inexpensive electrical timer can control a fridge

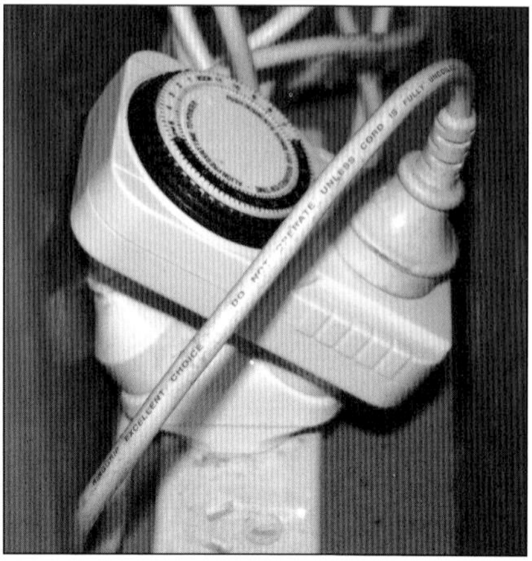

tech tip — **install a digital thermostat**

A Carel ir32s is an effective digital temperature controller for a wine cellar. It sells for around $160 from www.rs-components.com.au. See picture on page 64.

air flow

The next step in setting up your refrigerator is to ensure that the air flow is adequate to circulate the cool air . While some fridges have a built-in fan to cater for this, others may require more attention. A small $15 desk fan from Big W worked well for me. This can be wired by an electrician to operate when the thermostat turns on. Placing the fan near the cooling unit such that it creates an air flow throughout the cabinet helps to ensure even dissipation of cool air. Even with this in place, I have found that my unit maintains a constant bottle temperature of 12°C at the top near the cooling unit, 16°C half-way down and 19°C at the bottom. This performance is similar to that of equivalent commercial wine storage cabinets. Not perfect, but not bad, and given that the temperatures are stable on each level, this is effective enough for medium-term cellaring.

a "jiffy" box is a handy way to mount a thermostat

A fridge cellar can satisfy five of our seven conditions for ideal cellaring: a reasonably stable temperature, a low temperature, darkness, low ventilation and odour. See page 65 for strategies for controlling humidity. When it comes to establishing a more stable environment for serious cellaring, slightly more advanced options need to be brought into play.

fridge cellar stats

total cost	$240
capacity	120 bottles
cost per bottle	$2
running cost	~$15/year
construction time	1 afternoon

the drinks fridge

previous pages: Tahbilk cellar, Nagambie Lakes

How big should you make your cellar? The simple answer is, twice as big as you think you should! Every time I construct a bigger cellar it seems to fill faster than I expect. To calculate the number of bottles you need to keep on hand, multiply the number that you drink every year by the average number of years that you expect to keep them. For instance, if you drink half your wines straight away and the other half at six years of age, the average is three years. If you drink two bottles each week, that's 100 every year, so you'll need a cellar for 300 bottles (25 doz).

number of bottles in your cellar
=
number you drink every year
x
average number of years you intend to cellar each bottle

You won't get 300 bottles into a standard fridge, so it's time to step up. One option is a drinks fridge, like the ones that hold soft drinks and juice in service stations and convenience stores. Second-hand, these usually sell for around $1000 from commercial dealers, but you can pick them up for under $500 from time to time. They vary in size from one to four doors, with a capacity of something like 100-130 bottles per door. My two-door unit cost $450 and holds 250 bottles. The modifications are a little more involved than for a domestic fridge, but you'll end up with a better result.

tech tip — install a relay

A drinks fridge requires a new thermostat to be fitted by an electrician (see page 46). These units generally draw more current than a standard fridge, which may be more than the thermostat can handle. If in doubt, ask your electrician. An AC "relay" will solve the problem. The thermostat will turn the relay on and off, which in turn controls the refrigerator. RS Components sells a $20 unit which works well.

racking system

The larger your cellar cabinet, the more flexibility you will have for a more convenient racking system. The wire shelves in most commercial drinks fridges are more than rigid enough to support dozens of bottles,

a drinks fridge can be transformed into a great cellar

but the size of the shelves can make it difficult to access them without disturbing a stack of others.

Single bottle racking systems allow access to each bottle individually. The simplest and cheapest of these can be constructed from concrete reinforcing mesh. ARC Smorgon (www.smorgonsteel.com.au) sells a *Weldmesh* product with 4mm diameter wires welded into a grid of 10cm square holes, ideal for racking standard 750mL bottles. Two parallel sheets suspended vertically about 15–20cm apart provide a sturdy and inexpensive racking system and facilitate good air flow around the bottles. *Weldmesh* with 20cm spaces is also effective, with the advantage of allowing for five standard bottles per space (see example on page 69).

tech tip — working with weldmesh

When buying *Weldmesh* for wine racks, look for the galvanised version to avoid rust and corrosion. A 3.0m x 2.4m sheet costs about $70 and can be cut to size using bolt cutters or an angle grinder.

To make the most of the space in a drinks fridge, set up the racks such that the bottles are stored two deep, with the back row accessible by removing a bottle from the front row. To make it easier for yourself later on, organise your bottles such that the back bottle is the same as the front one where possible. Offset the back row by exactly half a bottle width in relation to the front row (5cm in the case of 10cm racking). When the back-row bottles are placed in neck-forward and the front row neck-back, the tops of the bottles lie alternately alongside each other, thus reducing the required depth of the cabinet. This also provides the flexibility to accommodate the many variations in bottle size and shape that are common these days. Another method that could work is to use three sheets of *Weldmesh*, with the bottles placed in a similar fashion, but sharing the middle rack to support the necks. Unusually shaped bottles could pose a problem here.

While the *Weldmesh* is ideal for standard bottles, the holes are not quite big enough for some sparkling wine bottles and most larger formats like magnums. To allow for these, leave a gap between the top of the racking and the top of the fridge. This provides space to stack a couple of rows of oversized bottles. Such an allowance may prove to be essential anyway, since the height of the doors through which you will need to install the racks is likely to be smaller than the interior height of the cabinet.

To attach the racks, construct timber

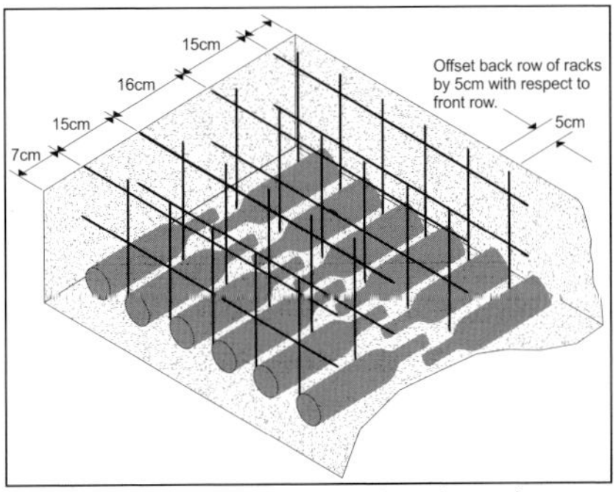

overlapping bottle necks make efficient use of space

a space above a rack provides for large format bottles

frames to run around the outside of each sheet of *Weldmesh*. 19x42mm pine will probably be the most economical option, and you should get by for around $30. Cut the *Weldmesh* such that about 19mm of wire protrudes from each side, which can then slot into holes drilled in the timber frames. Throw a coat or two of paint onto the timber to minimise mould build-up in the humid cellar environment. A very stable and professional-looking rack can be produced by screwing the frames together at the top and bottom around the *Weldmesh* and then screwing the whole thing into the interior of the cabinet. Depending on the depth available, position each pair of sheets about 15cm apart, with a gap of at least 16cm between the two pairs.

A simpler solution would be to screw the *Weldmesh* directly into the cabinet by alternating flat-head screws on either side of the sheets. If you go this way, I would still suggest running a timber support along the top and bottom of each sheet. This not only keeps them straight, avoiding the dangerous tendency of the racks to bulge outward, but it also provides more even distribution of weight at the bottom, and support for magnums at the top. Keep in mind that 250 bottles has a total mass of more than one-third of a tonne! A final option would be to weld the sheets into place - a good possibility if you have welding skills or a professional on hand.

darkness

Most drinks cabinets have glass doors, so it will be necessary to eliminate the light that enters the cabinet. These units also often have an interior light that runs continually. This will need to be rewired so that it can be turned off when the cabinet is closed (a simple job for an electrician). To reduce light through the doors, you could paint over the windows, but a more visually appealing option would be to tint the glass instead. Since ultraviolet light is the most damaging to wines, look for a dark ultraviolet tinting film. Car accessories outlets should have good options for around $30, and with a little care you shouldn't have any trouble applying it without bubbling. With the light on, you might be able to just see the bottles on the inside, assisting you in locating the right bottle without opening the door for long periods, potentially disrupting the temperature balance inside.

indexing system

There's nothing more frustrating than losing "that bottle" when you're in a hurry. If you have a couple of hundred bottles to sort through, an indexing system is vital. Label the rows numerically and the columns alphabetically like a spreadsheet. Stick-on vinyl letters and numbers from a stationery supplier are a neat and easy way to label each row and column. Each location can then be referenced next to each bottle in your cellar record (see page 75).

vibration

Commercial drinks cabinets tend to be powered by quite large compressors, which transfer a lot of vibration throughout the cabinet. By comparison, small circulation fans for assisting with air flow produce negligible disruption. If you can find a unit with the compressor mounted underneath (not on top), it shouldn't be too difficult to isolate it to eliminate the transfer of vibration. This can be achieved by supporting the weight of the compressor without relying on the frame of the cabinet. Unscrew the compressor unit from its base and cut holes with an angle grinder in the platform on which it is mounted. By making these holes slightly larger than building bricks, you can support the compressor on a couple of bricks or timber blocks. If you can get it to sit slightly higher than its original position, when the bricks are removed it can be screwed back into place for transportation. In its new position the vibration transferred to the wines should be imperceptible.

air circulation

With the unit assembled, it may take

refrigeration compressors are likely sources of vibration

some weeks to tweak its performance. In particular, the location of the thermostat and the level of air flow need to be optimised. It will also be necessary to bump up the humidity (see page 65).

On experimenting with different thermostat probe locations, I found the best position to be a little over half-way up at the back. In this location it was right in the air flow produced by the cooling fan. It would turn on frequently enough to maintain a variation of only 0.2°C in the bottle temperature, but not so often that the unit was forever turning on and off.

It seemed that the unit was functioning perfectly, but I measured a 5°C difference between the bottle temperatures at the top and bottom of the cabinet. My target was to get all of the bottles close to 15°C, not just somewhere between 13°C and 18°C. With the cooling unit at the bottom, the air was simply not circulating enough to adequately cool the top of the cabinet. The solution was to install a fan to increase the air flow.

The existing fan that pulled air through the cooling unit at the bottom was quite large and produced a stiff air flow. Worried that it was producing too much breeze, I had already suppressed it by placing a grille in front of it and rewiring it so that it only operated when the thermostat was on. It wasn't in a position to throw air right to the top of the cabinet, anyway. In order to achieve this, I mounted a smaller fan higher up that operated when the cooling system was off.

I purchased a 12cm rotary fan from Dick Smith Electronics for $40 and had it wired to the thermostat contacts that were active when the thermostat was off. Mounted half way up the cabinet, firing upwards, it proved to be effective in establishing a uniform temperature. In any given week, the bottle temperature varies by around 0.2°C and rarely ever more than 1°C. The seasonal variation is less than 2°C. Under these conditions, wines will mature slowly and gracefully for their maximum expected lifetime. The only limitation of this cellar is its capacity.

tech tip

install a fan yourself

To install a circulation fan without the help of an electrician, look for a 12V DC rotary fan. Computers use 80mm fans of this type in their power supplies, so you may be able to source one for nothing from an old computer.

drinks fridge cellar stats

total cost	$750
capacity	250 bottles
cost per bottle	$3
running cost	~$30/year
construction time	2 weekends

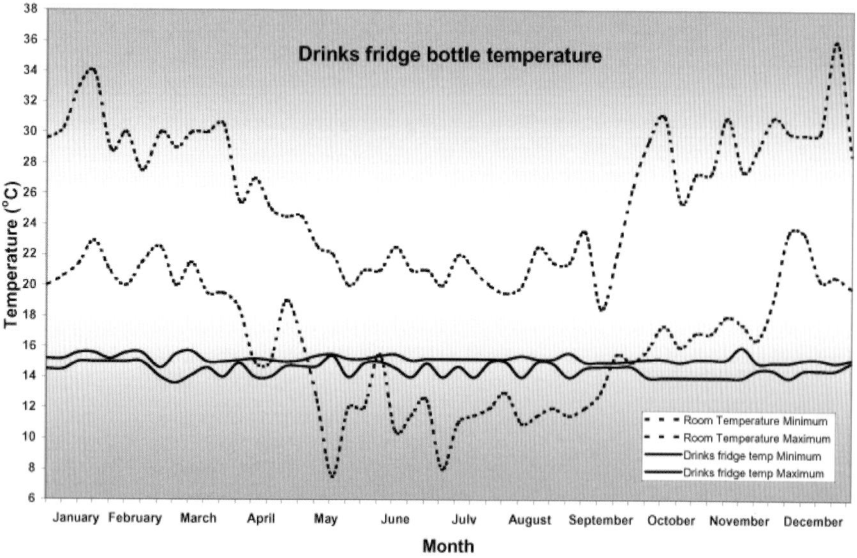

best cellar

I was eight years old when they replaced the floor in our Adelaide home. Weeks before it was dug up, I was active with a hammer, excitedly tapping the concrete around the house, hoping for a telltale echo of a hollow chamber that might indicate a vent - pointing to the existence of a cellar. The floor came up, and Dad covered over a section with an old door before the new floor was built. My brother and I waited in eager expectation until the night that Dad lifted that door and led us down a narrow set of century-old stairs to discover an ancient cellar.

I have been fascinated with cellars ever since, but a lot has changed since then. Cellars today are high-tech gear. Step into any of the specialised wine storage facilities dotted around the country and you'll discover pristine environments in which every detail is monitored 24/7 by sophisticated computer systems. If you're cellaring wine for a long time and don't mind having it stored off-site, a good facility like this is worth a look. It may cost a little more than doing it yourself, but leaving it in the hands of the professional saves you from worrying about the details.

Is a 26 degree temperature range really "temperature controlled"? Storage facilities like this one are unsuitable for wine storage.

These facilities also provide a seamless transition as your collection grows - unlike home options, where you need to trade up from one to the next. When you get above about 300 bottles (25 dozen), it's time to look at creating a wine room.

Some years ago I constructed a large wine cabinet for 500 bottles, which behaves in many ways like a small room. I wouldn't do it this way again (I'd convert a room instead), but the same principles apply.

The first priority in converting a room into a cellar is to ensure that it is adequately insulated. The key to both efficiency and stable temperature lies in effective insulation. If the walls are hollow or brick cavity and you have access to the inside from the roof, your task is a simple one. Buy a few bags of bean bag beans, and simply tip them in from above to fill the cavity. These can be expensive, but I found a nearby *Koolfoam* polystyrene factory which sells small polystyrene chips by the cubic metre for virtually no cost, so have a look around and see what you can line up.

If you don't have access to the cavity, you'll need to construct a false wall on the inside and insulate it suitably. This could work in a similar way to the wall in my cabinet. A frame could be constructed by bolting pine stud to the wall and filling the gaps with polystyrene foam (see diagram on next page). While refrigerators and commercial wine cooling cabinets use about 4–5cm of insulation, I went for 10cm thick polystyrene. The thicker the better. In addition, the less dense grades of polystyrene offer the most effective insulation and, conveniently, are also the cheapest. A trip to *Koolfoam* yielded (very large) off-cuts at half price. If the roof cavity is insulated above the cellar, add some more insulation to increase its effectiveness, as this will likely be the hottest area adjoining the cellar. If your cellar is on the bottom floor or doesn't have an accessible roof cavity above it, construct a false roof (in the same manner as the false walls) and ensure that it is well insulated. You will also need to cover windows, and sticking a neat piece of polystyrene to the back of the door will also assist in keeping heat out. Use rubber door seals to close all the gaps around the door.

In an attempt to reduce the transfer of both radiant heat and moisture through the walls, line the inside surface of the polystyrene with reflective "thermofoil". This proved to be too expensive for me at the time, so instead I purchased about ten rolls of the cheapest aluminium foil that I could find at my local supermarket! It's not as durable as thermofoil, but it does the job – and at less than a quarter of the price.

The walls and roof can then be panelled with sheets of timber. 4mm thick three-ply or marine-ply is effective and affordable. When it's in place, stain it to your preferred colour and give it at least a few coats of clear lacquer as a moisture barrier. The insulating performance of this system is excellent, and will keep a room at a fairly stable temperature.

In order to maintain a low temperature, climate control is a necessity in virtually all parts of Australia. While dedicated cellar cooling units are

a room or large cupboard can be custom-built for a collection of any size available, these tend to be very expensive and, from what I've seen, no more reliable than cheaper alternatives.

The cost of domestic air conditioners has plummeted in recent years, thanks, apparently, to the rising value of the Australian dollar. I picked up a 0.5hp (1.5kW) window-type Samsung unit for $225. It's a nifty little thing, one of the smallest air conditioners on the market, over-kill for my 500 bottle cabinet, but it would be well-suited to a small room. It's very quiet, hence good for indoor use and the air flow is gentle, so ideal for the cellar. For a larger room, spend a little more on a 1hp or 1.5hp unit. I've seen 1hp reverse-cycle split-system air conditioners advertised for $300. It seems they come up for less as soon as summer arrives every year (they'll be giving them away next!). Add a little for installation and annual running costs, and it's quite an economical solution.

Air conditioners offer a couple of advantages over fridge-type cooling systems in the cellar. First, by running a fridge at a higher temperature to that at which it was

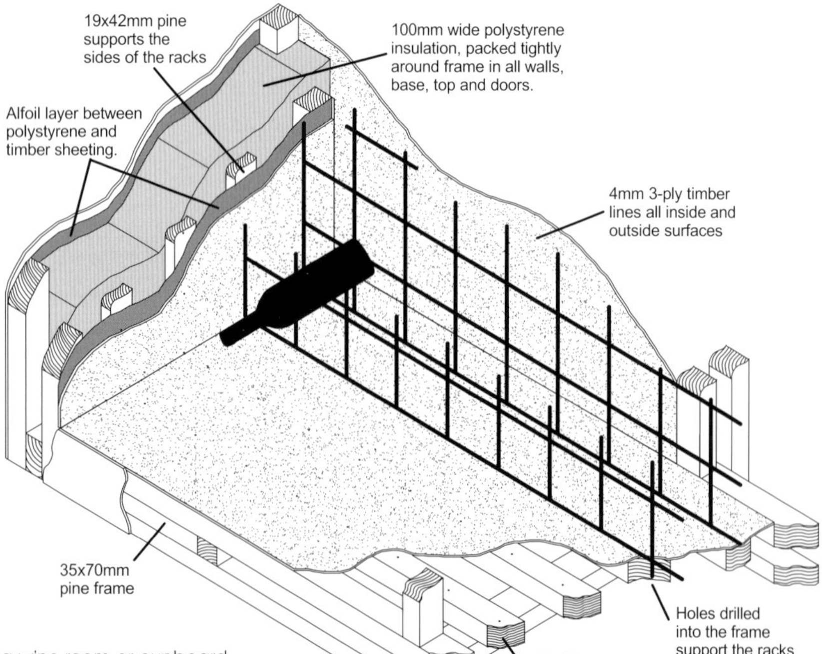

a wine room or cupboard can be insulated with polystyrene and alfoil and lined with plywood designed to run, greater pressure is put on the compressor. Given that cheap, second-hand compressors are not particularly reliable to start with, this is a recipe for burnout within a few years. Given the pittance that I've paid for each of my units, they owe me nothing by the time they give up the ghost. But when they do pack it in, I am faced with the cost of repairs. Compressors are generally replaced rather than fixed, and, at the costs I've been quoted, it would be cheaper to buy another fridge and start again. Not ideal.

An air conditioner, on the other hand, runs at a lower temperature in a cellar than its normal operating temperature. A window-type unit is also much more easily replaced than a refrigeration system as it simply slides into place as a fully-enclosed package – and for half the price. For these reasons, if you're at all serious about creating a decent-sized cellar, an air conditioner is your best friend.

Air conditioner thermostats usually have a range above about 18°C, so a new thermostat will be necessary (see page 46). Thermostat replacement on these units is a simple task for an electrician, and for a larger air conditioner a relay may also be necessary (see page 52).

tech tip

run an air con at 15°C

One of the risks in running an air conditioner at 15°C in a humid environment is that the evaporator (the bit that gets cold) can freeze over and restrict air from getting through, potentially destroying the unit. There is a simple way around this, and it cost me all of $4.50. Electrical timers are available from department stores and hardware shops. Look for those which are able to be set to "on" for 15 minutes, then "off" for 15 minutes throughout the day. By plugging the air conditioner into such a timer, even if the thermostat is on, it will always be off every 15 minutes for sufficient time for the moisture to condense and flow away. An air conditioner should have a condensate drain to allow this moisture to be carried off. Strangely, my Samsung unit was constructed without a drain, but this didn't take long to change (I have a good drill!). A brass hose fitting screwed and glued into place allowed a rubber hose to be attached to drain to a bucket. By mounting the air conditioner at a slight angle, the moisture flowed freely to the back and out through the drain.

Once the temperature is right in your cellar, it's time to do the inside fit-out. The final chapter will bring you up to speed on getting the humidity right. For lighting, choose

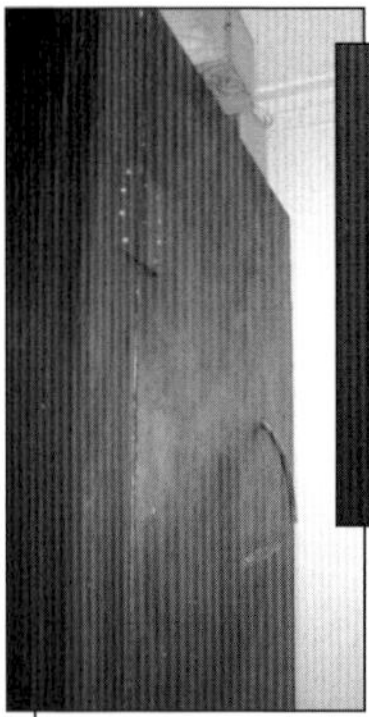

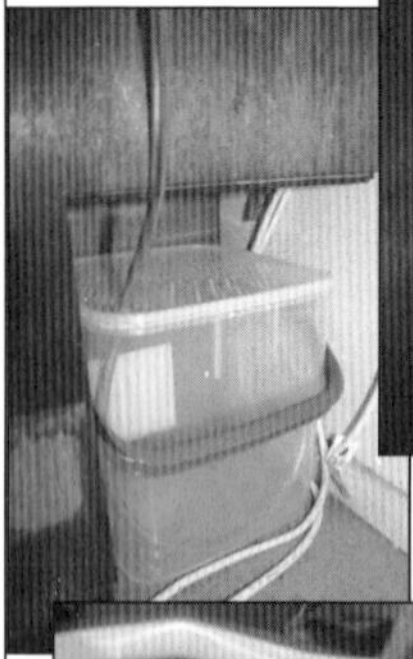

air conditioner installation

clockwise from top left

Cut a hole in the wall, through the insulation, slightly larger than the air conditioner. Mount the unit with a slight backward tilt and support it with bracing from the top and/or bottom. If it is mounted in a restricted space, use a small fan to assist with air flow. Install a moisture drain if one is not already fitted, and run the condensate to a bucket or drain.

a friend's wine room showing one of the many commercial racking options available today

an outdoor or moisture-proof fitting to cope with the high humidity environment.

There are many racking systems available for wine cellars from commercial suppliers. Most household storage shops also offer an ever-growing range these days. For single-bottle racking, the most economical solution is still two parallel sheets of *Weldmesh* (see page 53).

cold room

The simplest room-size cellar to construct yourself is based around a ready-made insulated room. Cold rooms are expensive to buy new, but can be quite reasonable second-hand. I picked up a 1.8m x 1.2m freezer room in good condition for $800 (see pictures over).

It needed a replacement thermostat and relay (see pages 46 and 52), so I decided to go for something different and try the Carel ir32s digital temperature controller ($160 from www.rs-components.com.au). I was looking for an excuse to road-test it. It hasn't missed a beat, but neither have any of my simple analogue units, so if I did it again I'd spend the extra $120 on wine instead!

For racking, I opted for a double-depth *Weldmesh* arrangement down each side (see page 53) as this provided capacity for some 435 bottles as well as space for a narrow walkway down the middle.

With the compressor system mounted on top, a significant amount of vibration would be transferred through the cabinet, so I built a frame attached to the roof of the car port above the cold room, to support the compressor. A refrigeration tradesman reconnected and regassed the unit and completed the electrical wiring when it was in place.

I replaced the door seal and latch to keep the cool air in, and after a coat of paint it was ready to go.

This cellar now runs at 12°C and serves as my white and sparkling wine cellar. Because of the power of the cooling system, the humidity in the cellar quickly dropped, so it was necessary to put in place a system to rectify this. The following chapter explains how to control humidity.

cold room cellar stats

total cost	$1300
capacity	435 bottles
cost per bottle	$3
running cost	~$50/year
construction time	1 week

A cold room is a ready-made insulated box which is easily transformed into an effective cellar with the addition of wine racks (above) and a thermostat (below). The thermostat pictured here is a Carel ir32s (see page 48). The cold room's original dial thermometer is also visible.

moisture matters

previous page: Penfolds' cellar, Adelaide

While it is obvious that a plant will die if it dries out, did you know that the same is true for a bottle of wine? The importance of maintaining the correct humidity in the cellar is second only to that of maintaining the right temperature. As we saw on page 19, about 70% to 80% relative humidity is ideal. Not too high, for fear of mould and peeling labels, and not so low as to dry out the corks. I have employed similar strategies to control humidity in all of my cellars. This chapter is dedicated to examining them.

While a stable temperature is more important than absolute temperature, the same is not true of humidity. It would be ideal for the humidity to be constant between 70% and 80%, but in reality a regular cycle of variation which fluctuates both above and below this range is just as effective. Adequate humidity is primarily required for the well-being of the moisture content of the cork. Under adverse conditions, it takes the cork some time to release this moisture. Hence, if the humidity varies from, say, 60% to 90% over a short refrigeration or air conditioner cycle, then provided the average humidity is correct, the cork will be happy. The consequences of high humidity are likewise avoided over such a cycle. Mould will not develop if the moisture level fluctuates rapidly, and labels will not peel unless they are damp for some time.

In climate-controlled cellars I have never encountered a problem with too much humidity. The natural dehumidifying effect of air conditioners and refrigeration units quickly sucks moisture out of the air, which must be replenished. Levels between about 40% and 60% are common – but quite unacceptable.

tech tip — humidity control

The solution to low humidity is to place evaporation buckets or trays in the cellar and to keep them topped up with water. In order to increase the surface area for evaporation, hang a towel in the water to act as a wick and soak up water which can then evaporate. The bigger the cellar and the more powerful the cooling unit, the bigger the bucket and towel. In my cold room, I use a full bath towel and drain the condensate from the evaporator straight into the bucket (because I can't be bothered refilling it by hand every few weeks!). A drain at the top of the bucket skims off excess before it overflows.

With this system in place, humidity now varies between about 65% and 85%, dropping to around 45% briefly when the cooling system is running. These levels are satisfactory for long-term cellaring as most of the time the humidity hovers between about 70% and 80%. Another option that is effective in very large cellars is to employ an evaporative cooling unit.

Controlling humidity is not just a

above, below & right: a towel hanging in water acts as a wick to draw up water, enhance evaporation and hence maintain humidity levels

matter of installing evaporative coolers or buckets with towel wicks. Humidity is influenced by a complex combination of factors: how long the cooling system runs, how much air circulation exists and how often and for how long the cabinet is opened. In raising the humidity levels in my commercial drinks fridge, I was faced with a more difficult task than in the case of my larger cellars. The powerful cooling unit had the capability of sucking a lot more moisture out of the air. This coupled with the smaller volume of the cabinet produced a very dry result.

In overcoming this, my first target was to adjust the operating temperature. Although I was keen to cellar my white wines at 14°C, by instead opting for 15°C, the cooling system ran less and the humidity consequently rose. Naturally, the running time is determined largely by the outside ambient temperature, so the humidity drops in summer and rises in winter. This effect must be taken into consideration when designing a humidity control system, and a means for continually tweaking the system to account for seasonal variation is desirable. For me, this simply means filling or emptying evaporative containers containing towel wicks. In the case of my commercial drinks fridge, I spaced three such small containers throughout the cabinet and included a large tray at the bottom in the path of the refrigerated air flow. All four of these are necessary in summer, but in winter when the cooling system runs less, I allow some to run dry.

Despite these measures, the humidity varied from only 52% to 75% in summer. This was still not adequate. An attempt to increase evaporation by plugging the hole that drained the condensate from the bottom of the cabinet proved to be impractical, as the water soon formed a deep puddle that threatened to engulf some unfortunate bottles on the bottom shelf! I needed to try a different approach. I had already considered installing a small fan to provide more even air circulation. By allowing this to run whenever the cooling system was off, I could achieve two goals by using it to also increase evaporation. I placed a container with a towel wick near this fan, and the humidity levels rose to between 55% and 85%, with an average around 75%. Perfect!

After a little experimentation, it is possible to bring even the most stubborn systems up to satisfactory levels of humidity.

the mould on the roof of Guigal's 300-year-old cellar in the Rhône Valley is a consequence of high humidity

final words

previous page: private cellar at Bethany Wines, Barossa Valley

There is something about enjoying wine with friends that can't be replicated with any other beverage. Wine unlocks food, it unlocks creativity, it unlocks conversation. And it is the cellar that unlocks the wine.

I have the privilege of regularly visiting winemakers and tasting wines while they are still grapes on the vine, fermenting in the tank, maturing in the barrel and waiting for release in the bottle. Before the wine reaches your table, it has already gone through quite a journey. The changes that it undergoes are nothing less than remarkable, but it might surprise you how unpalatable it can be at some points along the way, and how lifeless it can taste at other times.

Wines evolve through a series of amazing changes and these do not magically stop the moment it is sealed in the bottle.

Through economic necessity, many wines hit the shelves at a time when they are particularly lifeless or astringent. It is unfortunate that most of these bottles will be consumed in this state. But if you know better you will recognise the potential and give the cellar the time to unlock it.

In doing so, you are opening up a whole new dimension of wine enjoyment for yourself and your friends.

Starting with a small, simple cellar, the art of carefully maturing wine is a passion that you can enjoy for a lifetime. It can be achieved by anyone with a little initiative and creativity. Nurture a plant carefully and it will reward you.

Cellar complete, it's time get on with the business of drinking! You have the best bottles of your life to look forward to.

I wish you happy cellaring and many great bottles!

index

cellar record

The first step to getting the most out of every bottle in your cellar is to keep a record of how it's developing and when to drink it. This also doubles as an inventory to help you keep track of a larger collection. Every time you open a bottle, write a comment on how it tastes, make a note of how many you have left and update your estimate of when you will drink them. Use the following pages to help you to get started.

Example

Annie's Lane Copper Trail
producer/label

Shiraz, Clare Valley *2002*
variety/region vintage

$ *49* *2* *1/1/07* *WineStar* *B14 front*
price quantity purchase date purchased from location in cellar

comments: *A big, age-worthy wine, drinking well now but will improve for a decade. Try again around 2012.*

producer/label

variety/region vintage

$
price quantity purchase date purchased from location in cellar

comments:

producer/label

variety/region vintage

$ price quantity purchase date purchased from location in cellar

comments:

producer/label

variety/region vintage

$ price quantity purchase date purchased from location in cellar

comments:

producer/label

variety/region vintage

$ price quantity purchase date purchased from location in cellar

comments:

producer/label

variety/region vintage

$ price quantity purchase date purchased from location in cellar

comments:

producer/label

variety/region vintage

$ price quantity purchase date purchased from location in cellar

comments:

producer/label

variety/region vintage

$ price quantity purchase date purchased from location in cellar

comments:

producer/label

variety/region | vintage

$ price | quantity | purchase date | purchased from | location in cellar

comments:

producer/label

variety/region | vintage

$ price | quantity | purchase date | purchased from | location in cellar

comments:

producer/label

variety/region | vintage

$ price | quantity | purchase date | purchased from | location in cellar

comments:

producer/label

variety/region vintage

$ price quantity purchase date purchased from location in cellar

comments:

producer/label

variety/region vintage

$ price quantity purchase date purchased from location in cellar

comments:

producer/label

variety/region vintage

$ price quantity purchase date purchased from location in cellar

comments:

producer/label

variety/region vintage

$ price quantity purchase date purchased from location in cellar

comments:

producer/label

variety/region vintage

$ price quantity purchase date purchased from location in cellar

comments:

producer/label

variety/region vintage

$ price quantity purchase date purchased from location in cellar

comments:

producer/label

variety/region vintage

$ price quantity purchase date purchased from location in cellar

comments:

producer/label

variety/region vintage

$ price quantity purchase date purchased from location in cellar

comments:

producer/label

variety/region vintage

$ price quantity purchase date purchased from location in cellar

comments:

producer/label

variety/region vintage

$ price quantity purchase date purchased from location in cellar

comments:

producer/label

variety/region vintage

$ price quantity purchase date purchased from location in cellar

comments:

producer/label

variety/region vintage

$ price quantity purchase date purchased from location in cellar

comments:

producer/label

variety/region vintage

$ price quantity purchase date purchased from location in cellar

comments:

producer/label

variety/region vintage

$ price quantity purchase date purchased from location in cellar

comments:

producer/label

variety/region vintage

$ price quantity purchase date purchased from location in cellar

comments:

producer/label

variety/region

vintage

$

price

quantity

purchase date

purchased from

location in cellar

comments:

producer/label

variety/region

vintage

$

price

quantity

purchase date

purchased from

location in cellar

comments:

producer/label

variety/region

vintage

$

price

quantity

purchase date

purchased from

location in cellar

comments:

producer/label

variety/region

vintage

$

price quantity purchase date purchased from location in cellar

comments:

producer/label

variety/region

vintage

$

price quantity purchase date purchased from location in cellar

comments:

producer/label

variety/region

vintage

$

price quantity purchase date purchased from location in cellar

comments:

producer/label

variety/region

vintage

$

price | quantity | purchase date | purchased from | location in cellar

comments:

producer/label

variety/region

vintage

$

price | quantity | purchase date | purchased from | location in cellar

comments:

producer/label

variety/region

vintage

$

price | quantity | purchase date | purchased from | location in cellar

comments:

producer/label

variety/region vintage

$ price quantity purchase date purchased from location in cellar

comments:

producer/label

variety/region vintage

$ price quantity purchase date purchased from location in cellar

comments:

producer/label

variety/region vintage

$ price quantity purchase date purchased from location in cellar

comments:

producer/label

variety/region

vintage

$

price

quantity

purchase date

purchased from

location in cellar

comments:

producer/label

variety/region

vintage

$

price

quantity

purchase date

purchased from

location in cellar

comments:

producer/label

variety/region

vintage

$

price

quantity

purchase date

purchased from

location in cellar

comments:

producer/label

variety/region

vintage

$ price

quantity

purchase date

purchased from

location in cellar

comments:

producer/label

variety/region

vintage

$ price

quantity

purchase date

purchased from

location in cellar

comments:

producer/label

variety/region

vintage

$ price

quantity

purchase date

purchased from

location in cellar

comments:

producer/label

variety/region

vintage

$

price

quantity

purchase date

purchased from

location in cellar

comments:

producer/label

variety/region

vintage

$

price

quantity

purchase date

purchased from

location in cellar

comments:

producer/label

variety/region

vintage

$

price

quantity

purchase date

purchased from

location in cellar

comments:

producer/label

variety/region vintage

$ price quantity purchase date purchased from location in cellar

comments:

producer/label

variety/region vintage

$ price quantity purchase date purchased from location in cellar

comments:

producer/label

variety/region vintage

$ price quantity purchase date purchased from location in cellar

comments:

producer/label

variety/region vintage

$ price quantity purchase date purchased from location in cellar

comments:

producer/label

variety/region vintage

$ price quantity purchase date purchased from location in cellar

comments:

producer/label

variety/region vintage

$ price quantity purchase date purchased from location in cellar

comments:

producer/label

variety/region vintage

$ price quantity purchase date purchased from location in cellar

comments:

producer/label

variety/region vintage

$ price quantity purchase date purchased from location in cellar

comments:

producer/label

variety/region vintage

$ price quantity purchase date purchased from location in cellar

comments:

producer/label

variety/region vintage

$ price quantity purchase date purchased from location in cellar

comments:

producer/label

variety/region vintage

$ price quantity purchase date purchased from location in cellar

comments:

producer/label

variety/region vintage

$ price quantity purchase date purchased from location in cellar

comments:

producer/label

variety/region vintage

$ price quantity purchase date purchased from location in cellar

comments:

producer/label

variety/region vintage

$ price quantity purchase date purchased from location in cellar

comments:

producer/label

variety/region vintage

$ price quantity purchase date purchased from location in cellar

comments:

producer/label

variety/region vintage

$ price quantity purchase date purchased from location in cellar

comments:

producer/label

variety/region vintage

$ price quantity purchase date purchased from location in cellar

comments:

producer/label

variety/region vintage

$ price quantity purchase date purchased from location in cellar

comments:

producer/label

variety/region vintage

$ price quantity purchase date purchased from location in cellar

comments:

producer/label

variety/region vintage

$ price quantity purchase date purchased from location in cellar

comments:

producer/label

variety/region vintage

$ price quantity purchase date purchased from location in cellar

comments:

producer/label

variety/region vintage

$ price | quantity | purchase date | purchased from | location in cellar

comments:

producer/label

variety/region vintage

$ price | quantity | purchase date | purchased from | location in cellar

comments:

producer/label

variety/region vintage

$ price | quantity | purchase date | purchased from | location in cellar

comments: